DESTINY CARRIER
The Praying Woman

OLUBUKOLA IYANDA

COVENANT PUBLISHING

DESTINY CARRIER: The Praying Woman

Olubukola Iyanda

Unless otherwise stated, all scripture quotations are taken from the Holy Bible, King James Version (KJV). Other translations and paraphrases used include, Amplified Bible (AMP), Amplified Bible Classic Edition (AMPC), ASV, NET, NIV, and NLT.

ISBN: 978-1-907734-59-5

First Edition, First Printing October 2025

Covenant Publishing
samadewunmi@btinternet.com

CONTENTS

DEDICATION

This book is dedicated to the glory of God and my biological children, Anuoluwa, Oreoluwa, and Ibukunoluwa.

I'm grateful for the privilege given to me by God, the Creator of the universe, to carry you in my biological womb and the womb of destiny as well. Your lives are a testament to the fact that God answers mothers' prayers.

Thank you for yielding to the Holy Spirit when He nudges you as a result of prayers said in secret. Thank you for obeying when it's not convenient and thank you for understanding even when it doesn't make sense to you. Thank you for your support, encouragement, and all your sacrifices, through thick and thin. Thank you for allowing God to use you to help me trust Him. Your reward will not elude you in Jesus' name.

May your path continue to shine brighter and brighter in Jesus' name. There will be no limits for you in life and destiny. You are unstoppable in Jesus' name!

ACKNOWLEDGEMENT

I acknowledge the Trinity- God the Father, Son and Holy Spirit. Thank you, Holy Spirit, for the inspiration to put this book together, I thank God for the grace and help I have received. Thank you, Jesus for Calvary.

I also acknowledge my husband Pastor Olawale Iyanda who encouraged me to start every Wednesday night mother's prayers which led to the putting together of this book. I pray that you will fulfil destiny in Jesus' name.

FOREWORD

I am grateful to God for the opportunity to write the foreword to this Holy-Spirit inspired book. As I read through, I could sense the inspiration of the Holy Spirt that birthed this book.

Every mother will desire to see their children prosper in life and fulfil their destinies and this is fully aligned with God's desire. God has great plans for every one of His creations, and as Jeremiah wrote, God conceives the great plans He has for everyone even before they were conceived (Jer 1:5). This means that every woman who would like to see their children doing great things in life and fulfil their destinies has a great and powerful partner in God.

This book teaches women how to engage in this partnership with God through prayer. Women as carriers, and carriers of destinies have a responsibility to pray for the period of their entire lifetime for their children to fulfil their destinies in God. As James wrote in James 5:16, the effectual fervent prayer of a believer in Christ who is living righteously has great power. So, women it is time to arise and to pray!

The bond between a mother and child gives rise to a great passion that can be harnessed in the place of prayer. A passion that can be guided by the help of the Holy Spirit to make prayer powerful and effective. And because we have a God who hears the cry of His children, women can be confident that passionate prayers, founded on the Word of God, will bring about transformation in their children's lives.

This book supports women who are eager to embark on the journey of prayer. It encourages, teaches how to pray, assures that God answers prayers and has practical tools to help women who desire to pray. There are many prayer points and supporting scriptures. It is my prayer that the book will bless all those who make up their minds to bow their knees in the place of prayer for their children. May you be blessed as you read in Jesus' mighty name. Amen.

Professor Lola Akin Ojelabi
School of Law, RMIT University, Australia
Pastor @ RCCG: Strong Tower Assembly, Melbourne, Australia.

INTRODUCTION

This book was inspired out of a burning desire for the next generation to be protected and delivered from the disaster that has plagued the world.

The glorious destiny of many youth and young adults is being hindered by the enemy. They are being held captive by sin, retrogression, stagnation, ignorance, lack of direction, complacency, laziness, depression and all manners of affliction.

Many feel hopeless, helpless and many mothers are perplexed and troubled, thinking all hope is lost. But the good news is that there is hope in God through prayers and especially the prayers of a mother.

> *"For there is hope of a tree, If it be cut down, that it will sprout again, and that the tender branch thereof will not cease" (Job 14:7).*

This book, inspired by Holy Spirit, will encourage mothers to pray and trust God for change, transformation, and divine exemption from the plans of the enemy.

In this book, I examine the role of a woman as a destiny carrier

Mothers and all those passionate to see the next generation fulfil the plan of God for their lives should carefully go through this book and take action by the help of the Holy Spirit. You will receive help from above in Jesus' name.

"The LORD is my strength and my shield; my heart trusted in him, and I am helped: Therefore, my heart greatly rejoiceth; and with my song will I praise him" *(Psalm 28:7).*

So, mothers, arise and LET US TAKE THIS JOURNEY TOGETHER. WE WIN IN CHRIST JESUS! GLORY HALLELUJAH!

- CHAPTER 1 -

The Woman as a Carrier

From the beginning of creation, God gave the woman a very significant role in His agenda for humanity. No matter how great, wealthy or influential a man may be, a woman carried him/her in her womb for nine months. A woman is the vehicle through which men are brought to life and later nurtured. This is a great privilege with an enormous responsibility.

A woman is sometimes referred to as a man with a womb.

I believe a woman has two wombs: the physical womb and the spiritual womb.

I also believe that every child has a great destiny to fulfil, and mothers have a huge role to play in the fulfilment of their children's destiny.

Every woman has a significant role to play in shaping what a child becomes in life with God on our side.

However, if a woman is negligent in performing her role as a destiny carrier and shaper, things can go wrong in the child's life.

As a woman, you are a destiny carrier. God designed you that way. You have the privilege of carrying a child, both spiritually and physically. This privilege does not start and end with carrying your child in your womb for nine months. It begins before the conception of your child in your physical womb. After delivery, you are also designed to carry your child in your spiritual womb through your heartfelt prayers.

The Merriam-Webster dictionary defines the womb as a place where something is generated.

Life is formed in the womb of a woman. This is a mystery that no man can fully explain.

"As thou knowest not what is the way of the spirit, nor how the bones do grow in the womb of her that is with child: even so thou knowest not the works of God who maketh all" (Ecclesiastes 11:5).

God created the womb of a woman to house and nurture a fertilised egg until the foetus is ready to be born as a full-fledged human being. HALLELUJAH!

The preparation that takes place in the physical womb includes feeding the foetus with the right food and nourishment so that it can grow into a healthy baby.

The spiritual womb of a woman, on the other hand, is where a child is prayerfully instructed, nourished, equipped and launched into greatness through consistent prayers, intercession and godly instructions.

The womb, therefore, whether physical or spiritual, is the place where a child is prepared and equipped for a fulfilled life.

By praying and declaring God's word over your children, they become divinely protected and nourished for a life of great purpose.

- CHAPTER 2 -

Woman, A Spiritual Destiny Carrier

> *"Who hath heard such a thing? Who hath seen such things? Shall the earth be made to bring forth in one day? Or shall a nation be born at once? For as soon as Zion travailed, she brought forth her children"* *(Isaiah 66:8).*

Whenever there is travailing in the place of prayer, there will always be a bringing forth. There will always be an expected outcome. This outcome brings joy. Woman, as you travail on your knees, calling on the God that answers prayers, you will bring forth greatness in the life of your children in Jesus' name.

> *"Oh, my dear children! I feel as if I'm going through labor pains for you again, and they will continue until Christ is fully developed in your lives"* *(Galatians 4:19, NLT).*

In life, things don't just happen; someone somewhere makes it happen.

In the verse above, Paul describes what it takes to be a destiny carrier for one's spiritual children. He says it feels like going through labour pains, which will continue until Christ is fully developed in their lives.

Woman, it is our God-ordained assignment to continue carrying our children in the womb of prayers until the delivery of their God–ordained destiny; until they are fully established in the faith; until they reach their goal.

When we pray, a godly life is formed, a battered life is transformed, and a glorious destiny is realised.

> *"Lo, children are an heritage of the LORD: And the fruit of the womb is his reward. As arrows are in the hand of a mighty man; so are children of the youth" (Psalm 127:3).*

> *"But Jesus said, Suffer little children, and forbid them not, to come unto me: for of such is the kingdom of heaven. And he laid his hands on them, and departed thence" (Matthew 19:14).*

That little foetus in the womb today is a great destiny tomorrow if well nurtured physically and through prayers.

I wish that mothers could see with the eye of faith into God's plans for the future of that tiny baby in their hands. Jochebed, Moses' mother, perceiving that Moses was a destiny child, protected him from being killed even though the king had commanded that all Hebrew male children should be killed at birth. She was not afraid or timid about it. She fought for the destiny of her son with the wisdom God had given her.

Woman, stand up for your children if you notice anything that threatens their life and destiny. Stop every work of darkness through prayers and by God-inspired actions.

You can also speak out for them where it matters. Do not allow words that are contrary to their destinies to shape their lives.

> *"And there went a man of the house of Levi, and took to wife a daughter of Levi. And the woman conceived, and bare a son: and when she saw him that he was a goodly child, she hid him three months. And when she could no longer hide him, she took for him an ark of bulrushes, and daubed it with slime and with pitch, and put the child therein; and she laid it in the flags by the river's brink" (Exodus 2:1-3).*

Prayer Points

- Father, open my eyes to see who my seeds are and give me the strategy for their life-preservation, in Jesus' name. AMEN

The enemy saw that God was raising Moses as a saviour to deliver the Israelites from bondage. He therefore made a plan to kill him so that his destiny would not be fulfilled, and probably so that the children of Israel should remain a little longer in bondage.

The enemy also tried to kill the children of Israel to stop them from multiplying as God intended.

> *"And he said unto his people, Behold, the people of the children of Israel are more and mightier than we: come on, let us deal wisely with them; lest they multiply, and it come to pass, that, when there falleth out any war, they join also unto our enemies, and fight against us, and so get them up out of the land. And the king of Egypt spake to the Hebrew midwives, of which the name of the one was*

*Shiphrah, and the name of the other Puah: and he
said, When ye do the office of a midwife to the
Hebrew women, and see them upon the stools; if it
be a son, then ye shall kill him: but if it be a daughter,
then she shall live" (Exodus 1:9-16).*

- Father in the name of Jesus, every midwife assigned to kill my children at birth will not be able to perform their enterprise in Jesus' name.
- Any midwife in the spirit realm waiting to devour my children when their glorious destiny is about to be birthed will not prosper in Jesus' name.
- Father, weaken the hands of evildoers, let them not be able to perform their wicked acts over my children in Jesus' name. AMEN.

Let us take a closer look at this Scripture:

*"And the dragon stood before the woman which was
ready to be delivered, for to devour her child as soon
as it was born.' And the dragon was wroth with the
woman, and went to make war with the remnant of
her seed, which keep the commandments of God,
and have the testimony of Jesus Christ" (Revelation
12:4).*

The dragon (which implies the devil) wants to devour as soon as a child is born; he tries to kill the child physically and spiritually. Not only that, he tries to stop the child's destiny by diverting, derailing or stagnating it.

All these can be averted when a mother prays.

*"But thus saith the LORD, Even the captives of the
mighty shall be taken away, and the prey of the
terrible shall be delivered: for I will contend with him*

that contendeth with thee, and I will save thy children" (Isaiah 49:25).

- Father, I ask that you save my children from the plans of the dragons of life in Jesus' name.
- Father, I stand as a mother, and I come against every activity of the devil and his agents to devour or wage war against my children.
- I decree that the dragon shall not prevail over the destiny of my child in Jesus' name. Amen.

When Herod saw that Jesus was born to reign, he made plans to kill Him so He wouldn't be able to fulfil His purpose on earth.

"And when they were departed, behold, the angel of the Lord appeareth to Joseph in a dream, saying, Arise, and take the young child and his mother, and flee into Egypt, and be thou there until I bring thee word: for Herod will seek the young child to destroy him. and was there until the death of Herod: that it might be fulfilled which was spoken of the Lord by the prophet, saying, Out of Egypt have I called my son. Then Herod, when he saw that he was mocked of the wise men, was exceeding wroth, and sent forth, and slew all the children that were in Bethlehem, and in all the coasts thereof, from two years old and under, according to the time which he had diligently enquired of the wise men" (Matthew 2:13-16).

It is the purpose of God for our children to rule and reign on earth, so pray:

- Father, I ask that you frustrate the agenda of any form of Herod and every agent of darkness that wants to terminate the purpose of God for my children in Jesus' name.

- My children will not be victims of any evil decree in Jesus' name. AMEN.

- Father, I ask that my children rule and reign according to your purpose for them in Jesus' name.

- CHAPTER 3 -

The Single Woman As A Destiny Carrier

Everyone created by God with a womb is a woman, irrespective of your marital status.

A single woman who trusts God to be married has a responsibility to pray during her waiting season. They have a responsibility to pray ahead.

Although Hannah was married, she prayed ahead of Samuel's birth. No wonder she had a great outcome. Pray that your life will align with God's agenda. You can pray these prayers ahead of time, before you get married, and even before you know who you will marry.

Here are some prayer points for you as a single woman.

> *"And the LORD God said, it is not good that the man should be alone; I will make him an help meet for him" (Genesis 2:18).*

- Father, I thank you for creating me for a purpose (Jeremiah 29:11).
- Father, I yield myself to you, please prepare me in this season to be an effective and efficient helper for my husband.

- Father, by your Spirit, direct and lead me into your purpose for my life.

  "I will instruct thee and teach thee in the way which thou shalt go: I will guide thee with mine eye." Psalm 32:8

- Father, help my future husband to locate me according to your divine will and give me discernment of Spirit to recognise him in Jesus' name.

  "Whoso findeth a wife findeth a good thing, and obtaineth favour of the LORD" (Proverbs 18:22, KJV).

- Father, let the potential you have put in me begin to manifest.
- Father, let me continually be the good thing in my husband's life.

  "There shall nothing cast their young, nor be barren, in thy land: the number of thy days I will fulfil" (Exodus 23:26).

- Father, I ask in the name of Jesus Christ that I will not be barren of ideas and in the fruit of my body in Jesus' name.

- CHAPTER 4 -

The Assignment

The child God gave you is not an accident, even if you did not plan their birth. That child was planned and divinely orchestrated by God and should be nurtured with care.

The gender, race and circumstances around your child's conception and birth were deliberately planned by God to enable that child to fulfil a divine purpose here on earth.

The devil is not ignorant of this, and that is why he wages war against the seed of the woman, but in the name that is above every other name, the name of Jesus, the devil will not prevail over your seed.

> *"And the dragon was wroth with the woman, and went to make war with the remnant of her seed, which keep the commandments of God, and have the testimony of Jesus Christ" (Revelation 12:17).*

The devil hates women for so many reasons and has always been after the woman and her seed.

For instance, there was no record or reference made to the serpent having a conversation with Adam before Eve arrived on the scene. Adam had been in the Garden of Eden before Eve was formed, but the serpent only showed up in a conversation when Eve arrived.

Also, God loves women. No woman in the Bible cried out to God for help or trusted in God on any matter that God did not have compassion on and answer their prayers.

The Bible says we are gods, and that includes women.

> *"Jesus answered them, Is it not written in your law, I said, Ye are gods?" (John 10:34).*

I am therefore persuaded that God will show up in the life of every woman reading this book. He will vindicate you. AMEN

As a mother, you have a responsibility in the fulfilment of God's purpose for your child. A mother's responsibility as a destiny carrier starts before the child is conceived in the womb and does not end until the woman goes into the grave at a good old age. It is a lifelong responsibility.

Woman, congratulations, you are a privileged handiwork of God.

This responsibility is enormous and requires physical and spiritual capacity. Woman, you need to build the capacity to carry this colossal responsibility successfully.

Make these declarations:

> *The adversary will not prevail against my seeds in the exalted name of Jesus. AMEN.*

It is important to note that women are not to control or manipulate their children but to partner with God to support them so that they can fulfil their God given purpose on earth and ultimately make heaven.

Prayer Points

- Father, in the name of Jesus, I thank you for entrusting great destinies into my care. (Mention the names of both your biological and spiritual children.) I am grateful. I apologise for my complaints and murmurs in my role as a mother.
- Lord, please help me to fit into the purpose you have called me to in Jesus' name.
- Father, in the name of Jesus, please let me realise that you have equipped me with what it takes to fulfil my purpose as ordained by you in the lives of my children. AMEN.

Faithfulness on the part of a mother in fulfilling this assignment is required.

> *"Now it is required that those who have been given a trust must prove faithful" (1 Corinthians 4:2, NIV).*

- Father, please help me to be faithful in this role as a woman till a perfect old age.

For mothers who feel discouraged at the way things are playing out in the lives of their children, please be encouraged, for the Bible says,

> *"For surely there is an end; And thine expectation shall not be cut off" (Proverbs 23:18).*

One of the graces that God has given women is that we don't give up easily. If we believe in something, we will be committed to the cause for as long as it takes to achieve our desired result. An example is the woman of Canaan in Matthew 15:22-28.

> *"And, behold, a woman of Canaan came out of the same coasts, and cried unto him, saying, Have mercy on me, O Lord, thou Son of David; my daughter is grievously vexed with a devil. But he*

*answered her not a word. And his disciples came
and besought him, saying, Send her away; for she
crieth after us. But he answered and said, I am not
sent but unto the lost sheep of the house of Israel.
Then came she and worshipped him, saying, Lord,
help me. But he answered and said, It is not meet to
take the children's bread, and to cast it to dogs. Then
Jesus answered and said unto her, O woman, great is
thy faith: be it unto thee even as thou wilt. And her
daughter was made whole from that very hour."*

- Father, I trust you for a supernatural turnaround in the life of my children. Lord, please intervene and let my expectations of a great, fulfilled, and settled life for my children be a reality in Jesus' name.
- Father, I receive the grace not to give up in any situation.

> *"One day Jesus told his disciples a story to show that
> they should always pray and never give up" (Luke
> 18:1, NLT).*

Are you waiting on God for a child?

Never think it is impossible because you can do all things through Christ.

> *"I can do all things through Christ which
> strengtheneth me" (Philippians 4:13).*

If you don't have a child yet due to medical complications, loss of your womb or for any other reason, choose to believe God's report. The Bible says;

> *"And ye are complete in him, which is the head of all
> principality and power" (Colossians 2:10).*

It is never too late for God to show up.

- I pray for you in the name of the Lord God of hosts, receive a brand-new womb in Jesus' name.
- I command that medical condition to receive God's divine touch in Jesus' name.
- Every manipulation of the enemy regarding your fruitfulness is hereby cancelled in Jesus' name.

Go and bring forth your biological children. By this time next year embrace your child in Jesus' name.

Start praying Hannah's prayer. The Bible says,

> *"And her adversary also provoked her sore, for to make her fret, because the LORD had shut up her womb. So Hannah rose up after they had eaten in Shiloh, and after they had drunk. Now Eli the priest sat upon a seat by a post of the temple of the LORD. And she was in bitterness of soul, and prayed unto the LORD, and wept sore. And she vowed a vow, and said, O LORD of hosts, if thou wilt indeed look on the affliction of thine handmaid, and remember me, and not forget thine handmaid, but wilt give unto thine handmaid a man child, then I will give him unto the LORD all the days of his life, and there shall no razor come upon his head. And it came to pass, as she continued praying before the LORD, that Eli marked her mouth" (1 Samuel 1:6, 9-12).*

> *"Hitherto have ye asked nothing in my name: ask, and ye shall receive, that your joy may be full" (John 16:24).*

Hannah continued praying until she gave birth to her son; she prayed until her joy was complete. So, woman, don't quit praying if you are waiting for a child. Don't be discouraged. Continue to ask God until your joy is complete.

"There shall nothing cast their young, nor be barren, in thy land: the number of thy days I will fulfil" (Exodus 23:26).

"Sing, O barren, thou that didst not bear; break forth into singing, and cry aloud, thou that didst not travail with child: for more are the children of the desolate than the children of the married wife, saith the LORD. Enlarge the place of thy tent, and let them stretch forth the curtains of thine habitations: spare not, lengthen thy cords, and strengthen thy stakes; for thou shalt break forth on the right hand and on the left; and thy seed shall inherit the Gentiles, and make the desolate cities to be inhabited" (Isaiah 54:1-3).

These are the promises of God to you, dear daughter of Zion. Believe in God, keep confessing His Word, and you will experience the manifestations in your life in Jesus' name.

"The day will come, says the Lord, when I will do for Israel and Judah all the good things I have promised them"(Jeremiah 33:14, NLT).

- Father, thank you for your promise of fruitfulness. I ask in the name of Jesus that you will remember me this day and give me a child. Let my joy be complete in Jesus' name. Amen.

Write the date you prayed this prayer: (/   /   )

You will soon share your testimony of answers to this prayer in Jesus' name.

- CHAPTER 5 -

Woman, Build Your Carriage Capacity

Here, we are discussing your spiritual capacity.

What is capacity?

It refers to the abilities, such as strength and skill, required to perform a task, carry out an assignment or duty.

If you don't have the spiritual capacity, you can take a step today by establishing a solid foundation.

Every building starts with a foundation, and a structure that must withstand storms and floods must have a solid foundation.

The foundation for any spiritual building is the salvation of your soul. You must be born again. That is, receive Jesus as your Lord and Saviour and commit your life fully to God.

The decision to receive Jesus as your Lord and Saviour is the best decision you can ever make. This decision will not only affect you, but it will also affect your children.

Our choices as women will affect generations unborn.

"I call heaven and earth to record this day against you, that I have set before you life and death,

blessing and cursing: therefore choose life, that both thou and thy seed may live"(Deuteronomy 30:19).

Practical Steps to Receiving Christ

1. Acknowledge in your heart that you are a sinner.

> *"For all have sinned and come short of the glory of God"(Romans 3:23).*

2. Repent. That is, be sorry for your sins and be determined to forsake them.

> *"If we confess our sins, he is faithful and just to forgive us our sins, and to cleanse us from all unrighteousness" (1 John 1:9).*

3. Believe that Jesus came into the world to save sinners like you.

> *"For with the heart man believeth unto righteousness; and with the mouth confession is made unto salvation" (Romans 10:10).*

4. Ask Jesus to come into your heart by faith.

Please, pray this prayer for the salvation of your soul:

> *"Dear Lord Jesus, I come to you today. I am a sinner, but I don't want to sin anymore. Please, forgive my sins. I believe that JESUS CHRIST is the son of God and that He died for my sins. I believe He died for my sins and was raised from the dead for my justification. I therefore accept You as my Lord and personal Saviour. Thank you, Jesus, for saving me.*

Congratulations if you said this prayer. It means you are now born again, you are now a child of God. You now have the foundation for building spiritual capacity.

Start building on the foundation of your salvation.

These are the steps to take:

- Find a bible believing church and get planted there for your spiritual growth.
- Acknowledge the fact that you need God to help you.

    "Not that we are sufficient of ourselves to think any thing as of ourselves; but our sufficiency is of God" (2 Corinthians3:5)

- Be willing and prepared to pay the price required in building spiritual capacity, because things don't just happen. People make things happen as God gives them the ability to do so. The Bible says,

    "If ye be willing and obedient, ye shall eat the good of the land" (Isaiah 1:19)

- Be willing to pay the price by constantly and continuously reading your Bible, which is the word of God.

    "And now, brethren, I commend you to God, and to the word of his grace, which is able to build you up, and to give you an inheritance among all them which are sanctified" (Acts20:32).

The Word of God builds you up and strengthens your faith in God to trust Him for a great destiny for your children.

You discover in the Bible who you are and what you have access to by faith.

- Build a strong fellowship with God by praying always.

    "Never stop praying" (1 Thessalonians 5:17, NLT).

Pray against spiritual infertility. This includes, laziness in praying and studying of the word it is the will of God that you should bear fruits and that your fruit may remain.

> *"Ye have not chosen me, but I have chosen you, and ordained you, that ye should go and bring forth fruit, and that your fruit should remain: that whatsoever ye shall ask of the Father in my name, he may give it you" (John 15:16).*

It is therefore the will of God for you to birth a destiny. You may sometimes in your life's journey think the odds are against you but with God there are no odds, for with God all things are possible, whenever you feel threatened on your journey the response to threats is Spiritual warfare-PRAYERS

Push in prayers until your prophesy manifests.

> *"And I will put enmity between thee and the woman, and between thy seed and her seed; it shall bruise thy head, and thou shalt bruise his heel" (Genesis 3:15).*

As women, we have the huge privilege of carrying in our womb seeds that will crush the head of satan – whaoooo.

This is the way you should see the children God has given or is giving you. They will as one man crush the head of satan – hallelujah

So, whatever may be going on in the life of your children they will crush the head of satan they are destined to win in Jesus' name.

- CHAPTER 6 -

Assurance of Answers When you Pray

All glory to God, we are not praying from the point of fear or uncertainty or defeat.

God has assured us of answers when we pray.

> *"Offer unto God thanksgiving; and pay thy vows unto the Most High: and call upon me in the day of trouble: I will deliver thee, and thou shalt glorify me"* (Psalm 50:4-5).

> *"For I know the thoughts that I think toward you, saith the LORD, thoughts of peace, and not of evil, to give you an expected end. Then shall ye call upon me, and ye shall go and pray unto me, and I will hearken unto you. And ye shall seek me, and find me, when ye shall search for me with all your heart"* (Jeremiah 29:11-13).

> *"Because he hath set his love upon me, therefore will I deliver him: I will set him on high, because he hath known my name. He shall call upon me, and I will answer him: I will be with him in trouble; I will deliver him, and honour him"* (Psalm 91:14-15).

God indeed answers prayers. We have a word of assurance from Him that when we call, He will answer us, and as soon as we travail, we shall bring forth.

> *"I will answer them before they even call to me. While they are still talking about their needs, I will go ahead and answer their prayers!" (Isaiah 65:24).*

> *"So, let's not get tired of doing what is good. At just the right time, we will reap a harvest of blessings if we don't give up" (Galatians 6:9, NLT).*

Be encouraged. Don't give up on any child because prayer changes situations and transforms lives. Praying for our children is a good thing. It is the best gift we can give them, so keep praying and may the heavens over them, which look like brass, break open in Jesus' name.

Have faith in God

As women, we need to believe that when we pray, God is faithful to answer our prayers.

> *"Faithful is he that calleth you, who also will do it" (1 Thessalonians 5:24).*

I make bold to say that concerning the issues in the life of your children – GOD WILL DO IT.

> *"And blessed is she that believed: for there shall be a performance of those things which were told her from the Lord" (Luke 1:45).*

God is able to perform the things He has promised us in His word. The only thing required of us is to believe.

> *"While he yet spake, there came from the ruler of the synagogue's house certain which said, Thy daughter*

*is dead: why troublest thou the Master any further?
As soon as Jesus heard the word that was spoken, he
saith unto the ruler of the synagogue, be not afraid,
only believe" (Mark 5:35-36)*

Concerning that case that looks closed or dead,

DO NOT BE AFRAID ONLY BELIEVE.

DRY BONES CAN LIVE AGAIN- HALLELUJAH

Don't listen to what the devil is saying to you. Shut your heart to what that situation is telling you. Only believe what God is saying, exercise great faith.

What is great faith?

It is faith that perseveres. The kind of faith that keeps believing until the answer comes.

Jesus commended the faith of a woman in the Bible. Because of her faith, she received the answer to her prayers.

*"Then Jesus answered and said unto her, O woman,
great is thy faith: be it unto thee even as thou wilt.
And her daughter was made whole from that very
hour" (Matthew 15:28).*

Our children need to know that our faith is in God, and we need to encourage them to also put their faith in God. We must pass on the legacy of faith in God to our children so that, in old age, we will enjoy the peace of God.

*"To Timothy, my dearly beloved son: Grace, mercy,
and peace, from God the Father and Christ Jesus our
Lord. I thank God, whom I serve from my forefathers
with pure conscience, that without ceasing I have
remembrance of thee in my prayers night and day;*

greatly desiring to see thee, being mindful of thy tears, that I may be filled with joy; when I call to remembrance the unfeigned faith that is in thee, which dwelt first in thy grandmother Lois, and thy mother Eunice; and I am persuaded that in thee also" (2 Timothy 1:2-6).

Your children know you are praying. Do not fear; leave a legacy of faith. This is the most incredible legacy you can leave for your children.

- CHAPTER 7 -

Bible-based Prayers
for You and Your Children

I encourage you to keep a JOURNAL and note the decisions and steps you are taking towards your responsibilities as a Destiny Carrier, so that you can keep track of events and ultimately give thanks to God for the journey to answered prayers.

At the end of each prayer point, you will find a journal.

A) Prayer points for singles, newly married and waiting mothers.

God designed man to produce after His kind, and at creation, He gave a command that man should be fruitful and multiply.

> *"So, God created man in his own image, in the image of God created he him; male and female created he them. And God blessed them, and God said unto them, Be fruitful, and multiply, and replenish the earth, and subdue it: and have dominion over the fish of the sea, and over the fowl of the air, and over every living thing that moveth upon the earth"(Genesis 1:27-28).*

Do not believe the lie of the devil that says you will be barren. You may be experiencing a delay in having children, but that season of delay is not your end. You will surely have your own children in Jesus' name.

You are just at a bus stop in destiny, waiting for the arrival of God's promise to you. Therefore, prophesy to your body and womb that you will be fruitful, and you will multiply. Pray that you will never be barren according to the command of the Lord.

Prayer Points

> *"There shall nothing cast their young, nor be barren, in thy land: the number of thy days I will fulfil"* (Exodus 23:26).

- In Jesus' name, I will produce after my kind.
- I will not be barren. I am fruitful, I multiply in Jesus' name.
- In Jesus' name, I will not cast my young; my fruits will remain, and I will carry my pregnancy to full term in Jesus' name.

If you have been experiencing or experienced miscarriages I agree with you in faith that the last you had is the last in Jesus' name. No more miscarriages. AMEN

Journal

Date prayer was made _____

Bible passage _____

What God is telling me from this passage about my situation

_____

_____

_____

_____

_____

_____

What I am believing God to do in my life based on the Bible
passage

_____

_____

_____

_____

_____

What is the Holy Spirit impressing in my heart after praying

_____

_____

_____

_____

_____

What changes is the Holy Spirit impressing on my heart to make

_____

_____

_____

_____

_____

Date prayer was answered _____

B) Prayer of Thanksgiving

"Enter his gates with thanksgiving; go into his courts with praise. Give thanks to him and praise his name" (Psalms100:4, NLT).

"Give thanks in all circumstances; for this is God's will for you in Christ Jesus" (1 Thessalonians 5:18, NLT).

"By him therefore let us offer the sacrifice of praise to God continually, that is, the fruit of our lips giving thanks to his name" (Hebrews 13:15).

Prayer Points

- Father, in the name of Jesus, I thank you for the children you have given me.
- Father, in the name of Jesus, I thank you for the salvation of their souls.

  "But as it is written, Eye hath not seen, nor ear heard, neither have entered into the heart of man, the things which God hath prepared for them that love him" (1 Corinthians 2:9).

- Father, I thank you for the plans you have for their lives.
- Father, I thank you because your purpose for my children shall come to pass.

  "God is not a man, that he should lie; neither the son of man, that he should repent: Hath he said, and shall he not do it? Or hath he spoken, and shall he not make it good?" (Numbers 23:19).

- Thank you, Father, because you are too faithful to fail.

  "The LORD hath prepared his throne in the heavens; and His Kingdom ruleth over all" (Psalm 103:19).

- Father, thank you because you rule in the affairs of men, rule in the affairs of my children in Jesus' name.

Journal

Date prayer was made _____

Bible passage _____

What God is telling me from this passage about my children

_____

_____

_____

_____

_____

What I am believing God to do in the life of my children based
on the Bible passage

_____

_____

_____

_____

_____

What is the Holy Spirit impressing in my heart after praying

_____

_____

_____

_____

_____

What changes is the Holy Spirit impressing on my heart to make

_____

_____

_____

_____

_____

Date prayer was answered _____

C) Prayer of Dedication

When your children arrive, you need to dedicate them to God.

What does it mean to dedicate your child to God?

It means you are acknowledging that God gave you that child and you are committing your child to God and as parents you are making a commitment publicly to raise your child according to biblical principles and values and seeking guidance from God on how to nurture them.

Hannah showed us an example:

> *"But Hannah went not up; for she said unto her husband, I will not go up until the child be weaned, and then I will bring him, that he may appear before the LORD, and there abide for ever. And when she had weaned him, she took him up with her, with three bullocks, and one ephah of flour, and a bottle of wine, and brought him unto the house of the LORD in Shiloh: and the child was young. And she said, Oh my Lord, as thy soul liveth, my Lord, I am the woman that stood by thee here, praying unto the LORD. For this child I prayed; and the LORD hath given me my petition which I asked of him: therefore also I have lent him to the LORD; as long as he liveth he shall be lent to the LORD. And he worshipped the LORD there" (1 Samuel 1:22-28).*

What to note

Agree on a set time with your church to dedicate your child to God. It is important that you dedicate your child publicly, but this does not stop you from dedicating your child to God in the womb and at birth, immediately after the midwife hands over your baby to you. You can pray and give the baby back to God.

When you dedicate your child to God, you acknowledge God as the giver, and you are entrusting the child to Him to help you nurture them. It is an act of worship, an expression of your appreciation to God for the gift of the child. It shows that you depend on Him. It also means that you are entrusting the child's life into God's capable hands and that you are committed to raising the child in a godly way until the child is old enough to decide to accept Jesus as their Saviour.

Dedicating your child in church provides an opportunity to publicly make your commitment before God, your friends and family. However, Baby Dedication does not secure salvation. Instead, it is a symbolic moment of entrusting the child's life to God's will and purpose.

When you bring your children to be dedicated to God, you and your husband must live in obedience to the precepts of Scripture. You must be willing to be examples your children can follow in all manner of godliness.

> "Similarly, teach the older women to live in a way that honors God. They must not slander others or be heavy drinkers. Instead, they should teach others what is good. These older women must train the younger women to love their husbands and their children, to live wisely and be pure, to work in their homes, to do good, and to be submissive to their husbands. Then they will not bring shame on the word of God. In the same way, encourage the young men to live wisely. And you yourself must be an example to them by doing good works of every kind.

Let everything you do reflect the integrity and seriousness of your teaching" (Titus 2:3-7, NLT).

You can always make a fresh commitment to God if you have deviated from the terms of your dedication or if you dedicated your child to God without fully understanding what it means. You can always say Hannah's prayers at Shiloh, as mentioned in the above Bible passage.

Prayer Points

"For this child I prayed, and the LORD has granted me my request which I asked of Him. Therefore I have also dedicated him to the LORD; as long as he lives he is dedicated to the LORD." And they worshiped the LORD there (1 Samuel 1:27-28, AMP).

Journal

Date prayer was made _____

Bible passage _____

What God is telling me from this passage about my children

_____

_____

_____

_____

_____

_____

What I am believing God to do in the life of my children based on the Bible passage

_____

_____

_____

_____

_____

What is the Holy Spirit impressing in my heart after praying

_____

_____

_____

_____

_____

What changes is the Holy Spirit impressing on my heart to make

_____

_____

_____

_____

_____

_____

Date prayer was answered _____

D) Prayer for the salvation of the souls of your children

"When I call to remembrance the unfeigned faith that is in thee, which dwelt first in thy grandmother Lois, and thy mother Eunice; and I am persuaded that in thee also" (2 Timothy 1:5).

As mothers, we must be deliberate and intentional about passing on the legacy of faith in God to our children. We must start praying for the salvation of their souls; we must not leave it to chance but be intentional.

Start praying before they reach the age when they can decide to receive Jesus as their Lord and Saviour. Make declarations. Mention their names and declare that they will serve the God of the Bible. Declare that they will not serve God's enemies. By doing this, you are banking up prayers. Ask God to contend with any force that might want to contend for their salvation.

Be determined that they will be your converts. As soon as you know they have understanding, please preach to them.

"But thus saith the LORD, Even the captives of the mighty shall be taken away, and the prey of the terrible shall be delivered: for I will contend with him that contendeth with thee, and I will save thy children" (Isaiah 49:25).

Prayer Points

• Lord, save my children.

This should be the cry of every mother. When the issue of our children's salvation is resolved, many other things we are trusting God for in their lives will fall into place, and as mothers, we will also enjoy rest on all sides.

Kenneth Copeland shared the testimony of his salvation at one of the BELIEVERS CONVENTIONS. He said his mother continually and consistently prayed for the salvation of his soul. She had some of his pictures hung on the wall and kept praying over them until he got saved.

Pastor David Oyedepo (Jnr) also shared the testimony of how his mum led him to Christ.

See how these two extraordinary lives are turning out. All glory to God.

The testimony of your children's salvation and their exploits in God's vineyard is next in Jesus' name.

Woman, initiate that turnaround in the lives of your children; start praying today. Please don't give up until they are saved. It does not matter the age of your children, pray for the salvation of their souls. Even when they get born again, continue to pray that they will stand to the end.

> *"Never stop praying" (1 Thessalonians 5:17, NLT).*

> *"Oh, my dear children! I feel as if I'm going through labor pains for you again, and they will continue until Christ is fully developed in your lives" (Galatians 4:19, NLT).*

- Lord, make my children perfect examples of the believer.

> *"Let no man despise thy youth; but be thou an example of the believers, in word, in conversation, in charity, in spirit, in faith, in purity" (1 Timothy 4:12).*

Woman, you can make a change in your world by making a change in your home through effectual and fervent prayers for your children.

Journal

Date prayer was made _____

Bible passage _____

What God is telling me from this passage about my children

_____

_____

_____

_____

_____

What I am believing God to do in the life of my children based on the Bible passage

_____

_____

_____

_____

_____

What is the Holy Spirit impressing in my heart after praying

_____

_____

_____

_____

_____

What changes is the Holy Spirit impressing on my heart to make

_____

_____

_____

_____

_____

_____

Date prayer was answered _____

E) Prayer against life wasters and destiny wasters

"Let us go up against Judah, and vex it, and let us make a breach therein for us, and set a king in the midst of it, even the son of Tabeal: thus saith the Lord GOD, It shall not stand, neither shall it come to pass" (Isaiah 7:6).

"Thou shalt not be afraid for the terror by night; Nor for the arrow that flieth by day; Nor for the pestilence that walketh in darkness; Nor for the destruction that wasteth at noonday" (Psalm 91:5-6).

"And I will restore to you the years that the locust hath eaten, the cankerworm, and the caterpiller, and the palmerworm, my great army which I sent among you" (Joel 2:25).

Prayer Points

- Father, in the name of Jesus, I come against every agenda of the enemy to waste my children. Every attempt from the pit of hell to waste their lives, time, resources, talents and destinies shall not stand in Jesus' name.
- Every secret plan of the enemy to waste my children is hereby terminated in Jesus' name.
- The plan of the enemy to vex my children in their health, career, academics, business, marriage, relationships, etc., shall not come to pass in Jesus' name.

"Then Herod, when he saw that he was mocked of the wise men, was exceeding wroth, and sent forth, and slew all the children that were in Bethlehem, and in all the coasts thereof, from two years old and

under, according to the time which he had diligently enquired of the wise men" (Matthew 2:16).

- In the name of Jesus, my children will not be victims of any evil decree, circumstances or situations in Jesus' name.
- Every decree, governmental, ancestral, political, etc., targeting the glorious destiny of my children will not see the light of day in Jesus' name.

> *"And the king of Egypt spake to the Hebrew midwives, of which the name of the one was Shiphrah, and the name of the other Puah: and he said, When ye do the office of a midwife to the Hebrew women, and see them upon the stools; if it be a son, then ye shall kill him: but if it be a daughter, then she shall live" (Exodus 1:15-16).*

- Father, make a way of escape for my children. Let them escape from every evil decree planned to terminate or stop them in Jesus' name.

> *"And the space in which we came from Kadesh-barnea, until we were come over the brook Zered, was thirty and eight years; until all the generation of the men of war were wasted out from among the host, as the LORD sware unto them. For indeed the hand of the LORD was against them, to destroy them from among the host, until they were consumed" (Deuteronomy 2:15-15).*

- Father, in the name of Jesus, have mercy on my children. Don't let them fall into any error.
- Father, don't let your hand be against my children. Remember Calvary, remember resurrection and give me total victory in Jesus' name.

"Prepare slaughter for his children for the iniquity of their fathers; that they do not rise, nor possess the land, nor fill the face of the world with cities" (Isaiah 14:21).

- Father, show my children mercy. They will not be victims of the disaster caused by the sins and disobedience of parents and ancestors in Jesus' name. No disaster shall come to pass in their lives in Jesus' name.

   "He, that being often reproved hardeneth his neck, shall suddenly be destroyed, and that without remedy" (Proverbs29:1).

- Father, deliver my children from rebellion and stubbornness in Jesus' name.
- Every demonic Spirit that always says, "I will do what I like, no one can stop me", will not prosper in the lives of my children in Jesus' name.

   "Shall the prey be taken from the mighty, or the lawful captive delivered? But thus saith the LORD, Even the captives of the mighty shall be taken away, and the prey of the terrible shall be delivered: for I will contend with him that contendeth with thee, and I will save thy children" (Isaiah 49:24-25).

- Father, deliver my children from every form of captivity: riotous living, ignorance, disobedience, sin, bad friends, negative influence, and the inappropriate use of the internet and social media.
- Father, contend with every force that would contend with my children to harm them.
- Father, save my children. Let them know you as their Lord and Saviour. Let them have a personal relationship with you.

- Father, save my children from destruction in Jesus' name.
- I say no to life wasters: no to time wasters, no to destiny destroyers and diverters, no to devourers, no to the manifestation of anything contrary to God's promises in Jesus' name.

> "He also that is slothful (lazy, loose, slack, sloppy) in his work is brother to him that is a great waster" (Proverbs 18:9).

- Spirit of laziness and slothfulness, you will not prevail over my children. Lose your hold in the mighty name of Jesus.

> "Thou shalt not be afraid for the terror by night; Nor for the arrow that flieth by day; Nor for the pestilence that walketh in darkness; Nor for the destruction that wasteth at noonday" (Psalm 91:5).

- Every terror by night, arrow that flies by day, pestilence that walks in darkness and destruction that wastes at noonday, you will not prosper over my children in Jesus' name.
- Father, in the name of Jesus, blindfold every form of destroyer; they will not locate my children in Jesus' name.

> "For they came up with their cattle and their tents, and they came as grasshoppers for multitude; for both they and their camels were without number: and they entered into the land to destroy it" (Judges 6:5).

- Father, raise a standard against everything and anything that might have entered into my children's lives to destroy them.

Journal

Date prayer was made _____

Bible passage _____

What God is telling me from this passage about my children

_____

_____

_____

_____

_____

What I am believing God to do in the life of my children based
on the Bible passage

_____

_____

_____

_____

_____

What is the Holy Spirit impressing in my heart after praying

_____

_____

_____

_____

_____

What changes is the Holy Spirit impressing on my heart to make

_____

_____

_____

_____

_____

_____

Date prayer was answered _____

F) Prayer of Restoration

"And I will restore to you the years that the locust hath eaten, the cankerworm, and the caterpiller, and the palmerworm, my great army which I sent among you. And ye shall eat in plenty, and be satisfied, and praise the name of the LORD your God, that hath dealt wondrously with you: and my people shall never be ashamed" Joel 2:25-26).

Prayer Points

- Father, in the name of Jesus, whatever my children might have lost in terms of opportunity, time, position, job, health, etc., let there be restoration in Jesus' name.
- Let the transforming power of God transform the situation of my children from losses to surplus in Jesus' name.

Journal

Date prayer was made _____

Bible passage _____

What God is telling me from this passage about my children

_____

_____

_____

_____

_____

_____

What I am believing God to do in the life of my children based
on the Bible passage

_____

_____

_____

_____

_____

What is the Holy Spirit impressing in my heart after praying

_____

_____

_____

_____

What changes is the Holy Spirit impressing on my heart to make

_____

_____

_____

_____

_____

Date prayer was answered _____

G) Prayer for divine settlement and establishment

"But the God of all grace, who hath called us unto his eternal glory by Christ Jesus, after that ye have suffered a while, make you perfect, stablish, strengthen, settle you" (1 Peter 5:10).

"And let the beauty of the LORD our God be upon us: And establish thou the work of our hands upon us; Yea, the work of our hands establish thou it" (Psalm 90:17).

"Declaring the end from the beginning, and from ancient times the things that are not yet done, saying, My counsel shall stand, and I will do all my pleasure" (Isaiah 46:10).

"O satisfy us early with thy mercy; That we may rejoice and be glad all our days" (Psalm 90:14).

Prayer Points

- Father, I thank you for the good plans you have for my children.
- Father, I ask that your counsel for my children's academics and career come to pass in Jesus' name.
- Father, I ask according to your word, let my children be heads and not tails in Jesus' name.

    "And the LORD shall make thee the head, and not the tail; and thou shalt be above only, and thou shalt not be beneath; if that thou hearken unto the commandments of the LORD thy God, which I command thee this day, to observe and to do them" (Deuteronomy 28:13).

- Father, I ask that you settle my children financially in Jesus' name.
- Father, I ask that you connect my children divinely to the bone of their bones and the flesh of their flesh in marriage in Jesus' name.
- I decree my children will not miss it in marriage in Jesus' name.
- Father, I ask that you terminate every suffering, stagnation and delay in my children's journey in Jesus' name.
- Everything the devil has planned for their future is terminated in Jesus' name.
- Father, I ask that you will satisfy my children early with the good things of life.
- I forbid delays of any kind in their lives in Jesus' name.

Journal

Date prayer was made _____

Bible passage _____

What God is telling me from this passage about my children

_____

_____

_____

_____

_____

What I am believing God to do in the life of my children based
on the Bible passage

_____

_____

_____

_____

_____

What is the Holy Spirit impressing in my heart after praying

_____

_____

_____

_____

_____

What changes is the Holy Spirit impressing on my heart to make

_____

_____

_____

_____

_____

_____

Date prayer was answered _____

H) Prayer for children who are in physical or spiritual prisons.

"Lo, children are an heritage of the LORD: And the fruit of the womb is his reward" (Psalm 127:3).

"Though hand join in hand, the wicked shall not be unpunished: But the seed of the righteous shall be delivered" (Proverbs 11:21).

"I will answer them before they even call to me. While they are still talking about their needs, I will go ahead and answer their prayers!" (Zechariah 9:11-13, ASV).

Prayer Points

- Father, I ask in the name of Jesus that you deliver your heritage (my children - mention their names) from destruction.
- Father, I ask that you deliver my children from the pit where there is no water. Frustrate every conspiracy to keep them down and confined in Jesus' name.

  "And it came to pass, when Joseph was come unto his brethren, that they stript Joseph out of his coat, his coat of many colours that was on him; and they took him, and cast him into a pit: and the pit was empty, there was no water in it" (Genesis 37:23).

- Father, I ask that every garment of confinement on my children be consumed by the fire of the Holy Ghost in Jesus' name.
- Father, I ask in the name of Jesus, let there be a restoration of any garment of beauty and royalty that the enemy might have stolen from my children in Jesus' name.
- Father, I ask that you liberate my children from anything that wants to keep them in bondage in Jesus' name.

- Father, I ask in the name of Jesus that you deliver my children from the prison of sin.
- Father, in your mercy, deliver every child that has been put in prison due to bad behaviour in Jesus' name.

Journal

Date prayer was made _____

Bible passage _____

What God is telling me from this passage about my children

_____

_____

_____

_____

_____

_____

What I am believing God to do in the life of my children based
on the Bible passage

_____

_____

_____

_____

_____

What is the Holy Spirit impressing in my heart after praying

_____

_____

_____

_____

What changes is the Holy Spirit impressing on my heart to make

_____

_____

_____

_____

_____

Date prayer was answered _____

I) Prayer against vagabond spirit

Who is a Vagabond?

A Vagabond is a person who wanders from place to place. A vagabond has no home, no job, and so on. A vagabond roams about without any goal or ambition.

There is an adage that says, "The devil finds work for idle hands."

The word 'vagabond' is actually in the Bible. When God placed a curse on Cain because he killed his brother, Abel, he became a vagabond.

> *"And the LORD said unto Cain, Where is Abel thy brother? And he said, I know not: Am I my brother's keeper? And he said, What hast thou done? the voice of thy brother's blood crieth unto me from the ground. And now art thou cursed from the earth, which hath opened her mouth to receive thy brother's blood from thy hand; when thou tillest the ground, it shall not henceforth yield unto thee her strength; a fugitive and a vagabond shalt thou be in the earth" (Genesis 4:9-12).*

Prayer Points

- Father, in the name of Jesus, I declare that my children are not cursed; they are blessed. They will not be vagabonds in Jesus' name.
- I resist every vagabond Spirit. No vagabond spirit will have a grip on my children in Jesus' name.
- Father, I ask that if there is any sin my children have committed that deserves punishment, please remember

Calvary and the resurrection, and show them mercy in Jesus' name.

- Father, I ask that in your mercy, redirect and restore every child who has dropped out of school or has no ambition for vocation in life.
- Father, I ask that in your mercy, save and restore every child that has gone astray as a result of peer pressure, wrong association or cultism.
- Father, I ask in the name of Jesus that the Spirit of the wanderer will not prosper in the lives of my children.
- Every demon that makes a man move round in circles with no visible or tangible progress, lose your hold over my Children in Jesus' name.

Journal

Date prayer was made _____

Bible passage _____

What God is telling me from this passage about my children

_____

_____

_____

_____

_____

_____

What I am believing God to do in the life of my children based on the Bible passage

_____

_____

_____

_____

_____

What is the Holy Spirit impressing in my heart after praying

_____

_____

_____

_____

_____

What changes is the Holy Spirit impressing on my heart to make

_____

_____

_____

_____

_____

_____

Date prayer was answered _____

J) Prayer of peace

"And he arose, and rebuked the wind, and said unto the sea, Peace, be still. And the wind ceased, and there was a great calm" (Mark 4:39).

"He maketh the storm a calm, so that the waves thereof are still" (Psalm 107:29).

"Thou rulest the raging of the sea: When the waves thereof arise, thou stillest them" (Psalm 89:9).

Prayer Points

- Father, I ask that you speak calmness to any and every storm in the life of my children in Jesus' name.

Give them peace by all means in Jesus' name.

"Now the Lord of peace himself give you peace always by all means. The Lord be with you all" (2 Thessalonians 3:16).

- Father, I ask that in your mercy, give my children all-around peace. Let there be divine tranquility in their career, health, calling, marriage and every other aspect of their lives in Jesus' name.
- Father, I ask that every war cease.

"He maketh wars to cease unto the end of the earth; He breaketh the bow, and cutteth the spear in sunder; He burneth the chariot in the fire" (Psalm 46:9).

- Father, I ask that there be no trouble over my children. Let every troublemaker in the lives of my children be silenced forever in Jesus' name.

"When he giveth quietness, who then can make trouble?" (Job 34:29a).

"Thou knowest how that David my father could not build an house unto the name of the LORD his God for the wars which were about him on every side, until the LORD put them under the soles of his feet. But now the LORD my God hath given me rest on every side, so that there is neither adversary nor evil occurrent" (1 Kings 5:3-4).

- Father, I ask that this be the testimony of my children in Jesus' name.
- I decree and declare that my children will enjoy rest on all sides.
- David fought battles all his life, but Solomon enjoyed peace. Father, don't let my children fight the battles I have fought; give them peace around them in Jesus' name.
- I declare peace in my children's health, careers, businesses, jobs, and relationships, in Jesus' name.

Journal

Date prayer was made _____

Bible passage _____

What God is telling me from this passage about my children

_____

_____

_____

_____

_____

What I am believing God to do in the life of my children based
on the Bible passage

_____

_____

_____

_____

_____

What is the Holy Spirit impressing in my heart after praying

_____

_____

_____

_____

_____

What changes is the Holy Spirit impressing on my heart to make

_____

_____

_____

_____

_____

_____

Date prayer was answered _____

K) Prayer against anxiety

No more anxieties over my children.

"Do not fret or have any anxiety about anything, but in every circumstance and in everything, by prayer and petition (definite requests), with thanksgiving, continue to make your wants known to God" (Philippians 4:6, AMPC).

Prayer Points

- Father, I present everything that is giving me anxiety over my children to you, Lord, please take them over and glorify yourself in them in Jesus' name.

- Father, in the name of Jesus, I refuse to be afraid or anxious over the future of my children because I trust in you. I believe you have a glorious future ahead for them.

  "My times are in thy hand: Deliver me from the hand of mine enemies, and from them that persecute me" (Psalm 31:15).

  "For I know the thoughts that I think toward you, saith the LORD, thoughts of peace, and not of evil, to give you an expected end" (Jeremiah 29:11).

- Father, I thank you because the times of my children are in your hands. Thank you because you are a good God. You cannot mismanage their destinies, thank you dependable father.

  "But thus saith the LORD, Even the captives of the mighty shall be taken away, and the prey of the terrible shall be delivered: for I will contend with him

that contendeth with thee, and I will save thy children" (Isaiah 49:25).

- Father, save my children eternally, save them from every earthly destruction in Jesus' name.

    "And give him no rest, till he establish, and till he make Jerusalem a praise in the earth" (Isaiah 62:7).

- Father, give me grace not to give up until I see my children excel in life.

    "For the which cause I also suffer these things: nevertheless I am not ashamed: for I know whom I have believed, and am persuaded that he is able to keep that which I have committed unto him against that day" (2 Timothy 1:12).

- Father, thank you because you will do it. My children will fulfil your purpose in Jesus' name.

Journal

Date prayer was made _____

Bible passage _____

What God is telling me from this passage about my children

_____

_____

_____

_____

_____

_____

What I am believing God to do in the life of my children based
on the Bible passage

_____

_____

_____

_____

_____

What is the Holy Spirit impressing in my heart after praying

_____

_____

_____

_____

_____

What changes is the Holy Spirit impressing on my heart to make

_____

_____

_____

_____

_____

Date prayer was answered _____

L) Prayer for the delivery of divine portions

There is a good and significant portion allotted to your children in destiny. By the supernatural hand of God, they will take their portion in life in Jesus' name.

"This is the land which ye shall divide by lot unto the tribes of Israel for inheritance, and these are their portions, saith the Lord GOD" (Ezekiel 48:29).

Prayer Points

- Father, in your mercy and favour, let the portion of my children in life be delivered to them without fail. Let their portion in career, business, academics, marriage, job, etc., be delivered to them in Jesus' name.

  "But thus saith the LORD, Even the captives of the mighty shall be taken away, and the prey of the terrible shall be delivered: for I will contend with him that contendeth with thee, and I will save thy children. And I will feed them that oppress thee with their own flesh; and they shall be drunken with their own blood, as with sweet wine: and all flesh shall know that I the LORD am thy Saviour and thy Redeemer, the Mighty One of Jacob" (Isaiah 49:25-26).

- Father, in the name of Jesus, contend with anything that is contending with my children in their portion.

  "The LORD is the portion of mine inheritance and of my cup: Thou maintainest my lot" (Psalm 16:5).

- Father, in the name of Jesus, maintain the portion and lot of my children.

"And David enquired at the LORD, saying, Shall I pursue after this troop? Shall I overtake them? And he answered him, Pursue: for thou shalt surely overtake them, and without fail recover all" 1 Samuel 30:8).

- Father, any belonging of my children that has been diverted, stolen or destroyed, let there be restoration in your mercy.

  "Let them all be confounded and turned back that hate Zion" (Psalm 129:5).

- Stubborn pursuers of my children's destiny, desist in Jesus' name.
- Father, terminate every struggle, stagnation and delay in my children's lives in Jesus' name.

Journal

Date prayer was made _____

Bible passage _____

What God is telling me from this passage about my children

_____

_____

_____

_____

_____

_____

What I am believing God to do in the life of my children based
on the Bible passage

_____

_____

_____

_____

_____

What is the Holy Spirit impressing in my heart after praying

_____

_____

_____

_____

_____

What changes is the Holy Spirit impressing on my heart to make

_____

_____

_____

_____

_____

_____

Date prayer was answered _____

M) Lord, Remember My Children

> *"Remember me, O Lord, when you show favor to your people! Pay attention to me, when you deliver" (Psalms 106:4, NET).*

> *"But I am poor and needy; Yet the Lord thinketh upon me: Thou art my help and my deliverer; Make no tarrying, O my God" (Psalm 40:17).*

> *"O LORD, thou knowest: remember me, and visit me, and revenge me of my persecutors" (Jeremiah 15:15a).*

To remember means to keep in mind for attention and consideration

When God opens the book of remembrance, insults, mockery and reproach is taken away

> *"And they rose up in the morning early, and worshipped before the LORD, and returned, and came to their house to Ramah: and Elkanah knew Hannah his wife; and the LORD remembered her. Wherefore it came to pass, when the time was come about after Hannah had conceived, that she bare a son, and called his name Samuel, saying, Because I have asked him of the LORD" (1 Samuel 1:19-20).*

> *"And God remembered Noah, and every living thing, and all the cattle that was with him in the ark: and God made a wind to pass over the earth, and the waters asswaged" (Genesis 8:1).*

Prayer points

- Father, you remembered Hannah and took away her reproach, remember my family and terminate every reproach let every delay be terminated in Jesus's name.
- Father you remembered Noah and there was calmness and the ark rested, remember me also today and give me rest from all troubles let every rocking in my destiny cease in Jesus name
- Father, remember my household and show us favour in Jesus name.

Journal

Date prayer was made _____

Bible passage _____

What God is telling me from this passage about my children

_____

_____

_____

_____

_____

What I am believing God to do in the life of my children based
on the Bible passage

_____

_____

_____

_____

_____

What is the Holy Spirit impressing in my heart after praying

_____

_____

_____

_____

_____

What changes is the Holy Spirit impressing on my heart to make

_____

_____

_____

_____

_____

_____

Date prayer was answered _____

- CHAPTER 8 -

Testimonies of Praying Mothers

"The dawn of the great new movement of God repeatedly occurs in women's space"- Alastair Robert.

If we trace great men of God back to their beginnings, we will find hidden closets or lonely pews where mothers kneel in earnest and sincere prayers for their children. In the prayers of a mother, awakenings are born, people are won, idols are toppled, devils are undone, dry bones are raised, and prodigals are rescued. It's worth noting that before God laid His hands on a man, He first laid them on his mother.

Redemptive history turns on flawed but faithful mothers bearing great children: Sara-Isaac, Rachel-Joseph, Ruth-Obed, Hannah-Samuel, Elizabeth-John, Mary-Jesus Christ and Eunice-Timothy.

Of note among these women is Hannah, the weeping, anxious Hannah of 1 Samuel, Chapters 1 & 2. was not a well-known woman, nor was she particularly strong, but she was a praying woman, and through her prayers, God showed His great power. God heard Hannah's prayers and gave her a son. Her son, Samuel, established the kingdom of Israel (1 Samuel 16:10-13), inaugurated the nation's prophetic line (Acts 3:24; 13:20) and gained a standing by Moses as a mediator (Jeremiah 15:1).

In our present day we have the testimony of Mama Dodie Osteen of Lakewood church in Texas, United States of America a woman of prayer, how she consistently prayed for her children. Paul her son who went on a mission trip to Africa was plagued with malaria and dying, according to the testimony shared by Paul Osteen, his mother was alerted back home in the United States to pray for him, and it was at that point and time that his healing began to manifest.

Through prayer, Hannah's once barren womb gave birth to a son to rescue Israel. Instead of reacting to Peninnah's mockery and pestering, Hannah's anguish drove her to God, the God of her Strength. Her prayers moved the God of the universe. A mother's prayers can shake the world (1 Samuel 2:1-11). The God who crushed the serpent's head by the offspring of a woman has more victories to win. Jesus dealt the deadly blow to Satan; the blow no other son could give. As the enemy tries to raise himself against our offspring, we must take our place in Christ to crush the serpent's head. There is a need for a mother like Hannah, anguished yet open-handed, praying for her children.

A mother has a responsibility to pray for her children when they lack the words, understanding, or insight to pray for themselves. We must stand in the gap, praying for their salvation and their lives, just as the Holy Spirit intercedes for us. As mothers, we do a great deal to serve our children, but there is no service rendered that is more important than our intercession, because it is a powerful tool whose reach extends beyond our own.

Children are unique and have diverse needs, talents, and challenges, so there's no particular formula to follow when praying for them. Just depend on the Holy Spirit to help you as you intercede for them. Confess the word of God, His promises and prophecies concerning them. The Judge of the universe will not reject pleas that are in line with His word. He is capable of doing much more.

> *"Now unto Him who is able to do immeasurably more than all we ask or imagine, according to His power that is at work within us be glory for ever more" (Ephesians 3:20).*

Beloved carriers of destinies, let us come boldly to the throne of grace that we may obtain mercy and find grace to help in time of need (Hebrews 4:16) – Onibokun.

- CHAPTER 9 -

Woman, Be encouraged!

"Thus saith the LORD; A voice was heard in Ramah, lamentation, and bitter weeping; Rachel weeping for her children refused to be comforted for her children, because they were not. Thus saith the LORD; Refrain thy voice from weeping, and thine eyes from tears: for thy work shall be rewarded, saith the LORD; and they shall come again from the land of the enemy" (Jeremiah 31:15)

Woman, be encouraged. All your labour in prayers and every other way over your children shall be rewarded in Jesus' name.

"So let's not get tired of doing what is good. At just the right time we will reap a harvest of blessing if we don't give up." (Galatians 6:9, NLT).

Praying for your children and believing God that they will turn out well is a good thing. God is saying to you, don't be tired, keep at it. Keep praying and trusting God. Whenever you are distressed or discouraged about anything in the lives of your children, encourage yourself in the Lord and recover all from the enemy, just like David. Whatever the enemy has taken away from your children shall be recovered in Jesus' name.

"And David was greatly distressed; for the people spake of stoning him, because the soul of all the people was grieved, every man for his sons and for his daughters: but David encouraged himself in the LORD his God" (1 Samuel 30:6).

Keep holding onto all the promises of God for your children. They will surely come to pass even it may appear as though the adversary is gaining an upper hand. I am certain that with consistent prayers and trust in the ability of God to deliver, the table will turn in your favour in Jesus' name. Your eyes will see your desire over your children in Jesus' name.

Hear the testimony of David. God told him that Solomon will reign after him and David promised Bathsheba, Solomon's mother, that her son will be king after him, but Adonijah, without the knowledge of David, proclaimed himself as king.

"And Bath-sheba went in unto the king into the chamber: and the king was very old; and Abishag the Shunammite ministered unto the king. And Bath-sheba bowed, and did obeisance unto the king. And the king said, What wouldest thou? And she said unto him, My Lord, thou swarest by the LORD thy God unto thine handmaid, saying, Assuredly Solomon thy son shall reign after me, and he shall sit upon my throne. And now, behold, Adonijah reigneth; and now, my Lord the king, thou knowest it not" (1 Kings1 :15-19).

I believe Bathsheba must have been discouraged and lost hope at that point, but the table turned by divine intervention.

Woman, in that situation of hopelessness and discouragement, go ahead and bow in prayers to the King of kings and the Lord of lords and assuredly, things will turn around in your favour.

This is the testimony:

> *"And Jonathan answered and said to Adonijah, Verily our Lord king David hath made Solomon king. And the king hath sent with him Zadok the priest, and Nathan the prophet, and Benaiah the son of Jehoiada, and the Cherethites, and the Pelethites, and they have caused him to ride upon the king's mule: and Zadok the priest and Nathan the prophet have anointed him king in Gihon: and they are come up from thence rejoicing, so that the city rang again. This is the noise that ye have heard" (1 Kings 1:43-45).*

I announce to you, in the name of Jesus, you will rejoice again over your children, there will be shouts of joy and rejoicing in your household in Jesus' name. Amen.

David testified, you will testify too in Jesus' name.

> *"And also thus said the king, Blessed be the LORD God of Israel, which hath given one to sit on my throne this day, mine eyes even seeing it" (1 Kings 1:48).*

> *"Strength and honour are her clothing; and she shall rejoice in time to come" (Proverbs 31:25).*

Woman, your eyes will see God's salvation over your children in Jesus' name. Like the virtuous woman, you will rejoice after all your labour in Jesus' name.

- CHAPTER 10 -

Woman, Arise!!!

> *"In the days of Shamgar the son of Anath, in the days of Jael, the highways were unoccupied, and the travelers walked through byways. The inhabitants of the villages ceased, they ceased in Israel, until that I Deborah arose, that I arose a mother in Israel."*
> *Judges 5:6-7*

We must arise as mothers. Arise as a Deborah in your family, community and nation. Woman, you have what it takes so arise.

> *"Rise up, ye women that are at ease; hear my voice, ye careless daughters; give ear unto my speech"*
> *(Isaiah 32:9)*

We cannot afford to be careless we can't afford to be at ease when the devil is all out there to devour those great destinies that God has entrusted into our care.

GOD BLESS YOU

Join other women from around the globe every Wednesday to run the devil out of our territories in Jesus' name.

Destiny carriers' prayer meeting is held on zoom every Wednesday at 9 pm UK time in both winter and summer seasons. Please use the link below,

Web Link: https://us04web.zoom.us/j/7371990567

Alternatively, you can call in on 0330 088 5830. Meeting ID: 7371990567 and Password: 0804

God bless you

www.ingramcontent.com/pod-product-compliance
Lightning Source LLC
Chambersburg PA
CBHW040805150426
42813CB00056B/2651